RAILWAYS OF WALES IN THE 1960S

John Evans

First published 2018

Amberley Publishing
The Hill, Stroud
Gloucestershire, GL5 4EP

www.amberley-books.com

Copyright © John Evans, 2018

The right of John Evans to be identified as
the Author of this work has been asserted in
accordance with the Copyrights, Designs and
Patents Act 1988.

ISBN 978 1 4456 8255 6 (print)
ISBN 978 1 4456 8256 3 (ebook)

British Library Cataloguing in Publication Data.
A catalogue record for this book is available from
the British Library.

Origination by Amberley Publishing.
Printed in the UK.

Never Volunteer!

One miserable morning in late January 1968 we set off on a 180-mile drive to Porthmadog in North Wales. We had signed up for two days as volunteers on that greatest of all narrow gauge railways, the Festiniog. Arriving around nine o'clock, we joined a group of other volunteers at a meeting to determine our work plan for the weekend. The idea was to find something that best suited our practical skills, but as I had none, this was always going to be a difficult area. Eventually a couple of us were detached across the Cob – that impressive mile-long embankment over which railway and road run – to find employment at Boston Lodge Locomotive Works. As volunteers Bryan and I were less than ideal. I had no experience at all and he had ended up in Portmadoc Hospital on a previous attempt to offer his services.

The day is a bit of a blur due to my limitations with a tool kit; I am still not sure what a wrench looks like. The fact that we were not expected and no-one knew who we were also blew any chance of real achievement. In the end I did a bit of pointless clearing up in a musty old storeroom and then spent the rest of the day happily ferreting around the glorious old workshops and yards, where the treasures of the Festiniog Railway were maintained, rebuilt, and in many cases had been built in the first place. This was definitely the high point of my weekend. After a pleasant evening in a pub and a good night's sleep, we reported for duty the next day to be asked to paint a signal on the Cob blue (even now I can't imagine why) and then we drove home. This journey was enlivened when a deserter from the Army on a motorcycle and sidecar ignored a stop sign on the A5 and plunged into the side of my little red Fiat, effectively terminating its career, as it was never any good after being repaired. All my volunteering since then has sensibly involved pen, paper or talking, but strangely the Festiniog Railway has gone from strength to strength without the benefit of my physical participation.

There is nothing like the Welsh narrow gauge railways, as they nestle surreptitiously among rivers, hills and mountains, except, perhaps, the Welsh standard gauge. In this volume you will be treated to a healthy dose of both. It was rather ironic that at a time when the narrow gauge lines were giving encouraging signs of their vast tourist potential, the main lines were in decline. The old Great Western line from Ruabon to Barmouth Junction (Morfa Mawddach) had been dealt its death blow by Dr Beeching in 1965. The Cambrian line was still going, but express trains like the 'Cambrian Coast

Express' disappeared in 1967. The North Wales line from Chester to Holyhead was still very busy, especially on summer Saturdays. We will take a look at all these railways along with the nascent narrow gauge network. Recently I spent a week revisiting some of the old haunts I had enjoyed in the 1960s. The Ffestiniog Railway, now spelt with two Fs, is an amazing enterprise; I spent a whole day on it and yearned for more. The Talyllyn and Vale of Rheidol seemed less changed and the Welshpool & Llanfair now goes somewhere. The Fairbourne has changed its character completely and, oh no, the Snowdon line mainly uses diesels.

But the important thing is that they are all still there, and have been joined by a bunch of new interlopers, to provide even more fun. In fact there are now eleven Great Little Trains of Wales, one of which is entirely a misnomer as there is nothing little about the Welsh Highland or its rollercoaster history.

All that is for another day. Let's travel back to the mid-1960s, grab a roll or two of costly Kodak Ektachrome colour slide film for that Petriflex camera, and see what all the fuss was about.

John Evans
Luddenden, West Yorkshire
2018

The Festiniog Railway at Porthmadog on a grey day in January 1968, when Harbour station slept and the author was about to embark on his first attempt at volunteering.

Soul Survivors

Both Wales and Ireland were eminently suitable for the narrow gauge railway as difficult terrain and remote populations in need of a transport system meant that the cost of a standard gauge railway would have been prohibitive. The Festiniog, Talyllyn, Corris and other railways were products of the early to mid-nineteenth century transport boom, the former being notable as the inaugural passenger-carrying narrow gauge line in the British Isles. It was also the first to use steam on such a narrow gauge as 1 foot 11½ inches.

Creating a new railway was a tedious business due to the need for an Act of Parliament for each new line. To make things easier, the Light Railways Act of 1896 allowed a railway to be built and operated with just a Light Railway Order. Many of the strictures necessary for a normal railway were waived; for example, crossing gates could be dispensed with. The Vale of Rheidol and the Welshpool & Llanfair were both built under the Light Railways Act, as were many others in England. Most succumbed to road transport, but the Welshpool line made it through to the 1950s and the Vale of Rheidol had the dubious honour of being British Railways' only steam line after 1968.

In the 1960s, the Welsh narrow gauge railways were in different stages of either development or operation. The Vale of Rheidol was a British Railways line and had a completely different feel from the enthusiast-owned lines. The Snowdon Mountain Railway was a private business and thoughts of resuscitating part of the Corris or the Glyn Valley Tramway were simply impossible dreams. Enthusiasts of the 1960s would also have been unable to predict the creation of entirely new narrow gauge railways like the Llanberis Lake, Bala Lake and Brecon Mountain. Nothing could have prepared them for the reconstruction of the disastrous Welsh Highland, whose closure in 1936 both left a 20-mile scar across the countryside and hurt the feelings of anyone who invested in it.

This book makes no pretences about completeness; it is intended to give a snapshot in colour of the railways in North Wales in the mid to late 1960s, when the rosy future the railways enjoy today was by no means assured. We also take a look at the main lines as they said farewell to steam. After seeing some of the pictures in this book, a thirty-year volunteer on the Festiniog Railway said he could not imagine how it had transformed itself from something so modest in 1967 to today's ambitious national tourist attraction. I suggested that, like the other Welsh narrow gauge lines, the Festiniog's essential character and individuality had been retained. These lines have a soul. How sad that we cannot write the same account of the Irish narrow gauge, which has basically disappeared.

Running any kind of railway today is a serious business. Back in the 1960s it was also enormous fun and there were fewer people around. If you wanted to step on the footplate, it was never a problem – you might even get a ride. Wandering around old sidings and buildings was almost encouraged and this included Machynlleth BR shed, where a request to move an engine a few feet forward for a photograph would be greeted with a toot on the whistle and a friendly wave of acquiescence. I have used the names current in Wales at the time, as it seems more appropriate in what is a historical account.

This book would be the poorer without the help of Bryan Jeyes, who accompanied me in my youthful wanderings and contributed many photographs to this book. Unlike me, he was handy with a box of tools. I am also indebted to Ron Fisher, who was taking colour pictures way back in the early 1960s. It is a privilege to be able to use some of them. Like Bryan, Ron was a Festiniog volunteer. Pictures unattributed were taken by the author.

The Welshpool & Llanfair Light Railway

Something of a farmers' line, the Welshpool & Llanfair covered a distance of about 8 miles through lovely, undulating countryside, connecting the small market town of Llanfair Caereinion with Welshpool in the county of Montgomeryshire. The tracks then ran tantalisingly through the narrow streets of Welshpool, popping out from behind buildings to cross local roads on their way to the main line station. There was no great drama when passenger services were withdrawn in 1931, ironically being displaced by buses run by the Great Western, who also owned the railway. Yet the W&LLR, with its two sturdy little engines *The Earl* and *The Countess*, kept going when others fell by the wayside. Of course it couldn't last and in 1956 the line, by then part of British Railways, closed due to the convenience and lower cost of road transport. Even at the end it was still quite busy. A preservation society was formed, but initially made little progress, partly due to antagonism from Welshpool Borough Council. The council wanted to use the tracks in town for road widening, so the preservationists had to set their sights on running from Raven Square, on the outskirts of town. At last in 1963 the line re-opened, initially the western half from Llanfair Caereinion to Castle Caereinion. It took a further eighteen years to reach Raven Square, and there is now talk of completing the section within Welshpool using a new route. Presumably the council are a bit friendlier these days.

Happily, the two original locomotives have survived and the pictures show both of them at work. The original carriages disappeared in the 1930s, so new ones have been acquired from around the world. The gauge of 2 feet 6 inches is unusual in the UK and sourcing stock locally has been a problem. The coaches used in the early preservation days were Cravens vehicles acquired from the Chattenden & Upnor Railway, a military line also built to 2-foot 6-inch gauge and closed in 1961.

In the 1960s, it was a delightful line to visit. They could probably have done with rather more visitors, but in those days trains ambled through the undulating countryside, with the fireman stepping off the footplate to wave his steed across ungated crossings. The whole thing had a charming rural feel and time really did stand still. The group of enthusiasts who made all this possible were short on funds, but long on endeavour, and a visit in the 1960s was unspectacular yet very satisfying. It was perfectly okay to hop off the train and photograph it being waved over a crossing. The lineside was a bit overgrown, but the big signals lent the whole thing an air of authority. Severe curves and steep gradients meant the journey was leisurely, but if you were in a hurry you were in the wrong place. I visited again in the early 1970s and our train was hauled by a big French tank engine with Austrian coaches, a rather incongruous affair in such bucolic Welsh surroundings.

A rare colour picture of No. 822 *The Earl* in August 1961, shortly after returning from Oswestry Works to the Welshpool & Llanfair Railway, and seen here before being repainted. This was five years after closure and two years before services restarted. (Ron Fisher)

In August 1966 *The Countess* takes on water while the driver chats to passengers who have alighted to witness the proceedings. (Bryan Jeyes)

A train crosses the road near Castle Caereinion on the Welshpool & Llanfair Railway on 21 August 1966. If you asked nicely, you could get a ride in the cab of *The Countess*.

Here the train has stopped at a crossing near Castle Caereinion and the fireman is about to shepherd it safely across a cattle grid and an ungated road. The railway had been open for just three years, hence the rather overgrown lineside, which I think is quite appealing.

Early preservation days on the Welshpool & Llanfair Light Railway. A train headed by *The Countess* is seen here at a crossing near Castle Caereinion on 21 August 1966. The undulating, but very pretty countryside is quite different from that traversed by other Welsh narrow gauge lines.

This picture of *The Earl* portrays a nicely amateurish scene – a preserved railway a world away from some of today's highly efficient tourist attractions. The driver has his pipe and people are about to enjoy a pleasantly informal train ride. Note the lads jumping onto the tracks at Castle Caereinion on 13 August 1967.

The Welshpool & Llanfair Railway's 0-6-0T *The Countess* is seen here on 21 August 1966 at Castle Caereinion prior to heading back to Llanfair with its train, but business is a bit quiet on this Sunday morning. Three years earlier an enthusiast special gave this engine a last chance to use the Cattle Market station in Welshpool.

The two original engines on the Welshpool & Llanfair Railway are seen here at Llanfair Caereinion on 13 August 1967, with *The Earl* in steam and *The Countess* undergoing maintenance. The Great Western and BR numbered these engines 822 and 823, and only No. 822 was in use in the latter days of BR ownership.

We are now at Castle Crossing and *The Earl* rumbles by with its mixed train on 13 August 1967. The full-size Great Western-style lamp irons are a reminder that this was a former Great Western line.

The sun emerged from the clouds and brought a touch of warmth to this bucolic scene with *The Earl* waiting to leave Castle Caereinion. I seem to recall that you bought tickets from the first vehicle, a mobile booking office. 13 August 1967.

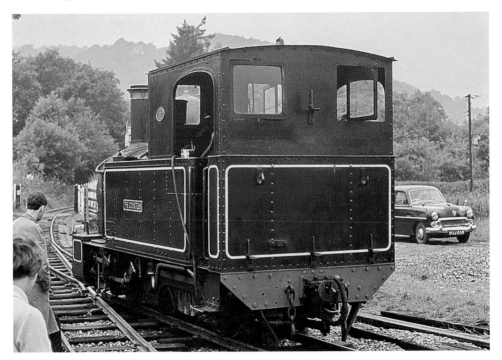

The Countess at Llanfair Caereinion on 28 August 1967 – it is sobering to think the lad in the foreground will now be in his sixties and the nice old Vauxhall would be quite a collector's piece.

The Countess has now reached Llanfair Caereinion in August 1966 with a full-sized signal looming over the coaches. This engine was painted in the railway's original lined black and has outside frames topped by some very Great Western boiler fittings.

A picture that captures the delightful rural feel of the railway, with *The Earl* rumbling through the countryside on its way back to Llanfair Caereinion in August 1967. (Bryan Jeyes)

The Talyllyn Railway

The Festiniog Railway touched your head and the Talyllyn captured your heart. Here was the epitome of a narrow gauge railway, with cheeky antique engines pulling dainty coaches that bucked and swayed as your train climbed into the mountains. Back in the 1960s there was no continuous brake, so progress was jerky in the extreme, but once you set foot on the platform at Towyn Wharf station, you entered another world. This was how you expected a Welsh narrow gauge railway to look. Turn right and the old red French locomotive *Cambrai* filled your gaze, together with a tall signal and overbridge on the adjacent British Railways main line right at the end of the platform. Wharf station, a modest structure with tall chimneys, matched the train perfectly. Oddly, when I returned recently and saw the big new developments at what is now Tywyn Wharf, the atmosphere seemed to be the same. Each departure was an event. And although it was not like the early 1950s, when the staff at Wharf station lived in hope that the departing train would actually return, there was a great sense of fun and anticipation. It felt delightfully informal and I suspect it always did and always will.

Part of this is down to the locomotives. *Talyllyn* and *Dolgoch* are now 150 years old, and despite lots of major overhauls and improvements to cater for changing times and heavier trains, they are still the real deal. It's a bit like William the Conqueror's penknife, which has had four new handles and two new blades. There were three other engines, two from the closed Corris Railway and one, *Douglas*, with a military history. They fitted in perfectly. Back in the 1960s, and also more recently, I found the trains full of chatty people enjoying the ride for no other reason than to enjoy the ride. Of course, you can inspect Dolgoch waterfalls and the old Bryn Eglwys slate quarries, but this is really a train ride in the best sense. It doesn't go anywhere important. Once you reach Dolgoch and Abergynolwyn, the scenery changes from the valley views present on the earlier uphill sections. These stations nestle in the hills and the classic view of *Dolgoch* taking water from the old stone water tower was one that attracted thousands of cameras. Part of the fun for us was examining the superbly restored ex-Corris Railway coach, or the two tiny carriages once used on the Glyn Valley Tramway.

The Talyllyn was created in 1865 to move slate from the Bryn Eglwys quarries and was worked by steam engines right from the start. Quite why *Talyllyn* and *Dolgoch*, which were both built by Fletcher Jennings within two years of each other, are so totally different seems something of a mystery. The line struggled on, latterly operated by local landowner and former MP Sir Henry Haydn Jones, but when he died in 1950 it looked as though the Talyllyn, in pretty dreadful condition and catering just for tourists, was finished. The story of how a group of enthusiasts rescued the line and ran trains is one not to be missed (see Tom Rolt's wonderful book *Railway Adventure),* but more importantly it created a template for the dozens of other railways, both narrow and standard gauge, that have followed suit. If you admire the double-track Great Central Railway and its fleet of huge engines, its inspiration is down to Tom Rolt and his friends.

Built to the rare gauge of 2 feet 3 inches, the Talyllyn's place in history is assured. The click of tiny wheels on rail joints will surely be a sound that generations of future visitors to the narrow gauge lines of Wales will continue to enjoy. Thank the Talyllyn for making it happen.

Towyn Wharf station on 22 August 1966 and the engine is 0-4-0T No. 2 *Dolgoch*, which was exactly 100 years old at the time, having been supplied by Fletcher Jennings in 1866. Note the abundant brass work, long wheelbase and contrasting refreshment coach.

This picture gives a good impression of the atmosphere at Towyn Wharf in 1966. Note the BR signal – the Cambrian Coast line runs just behind the Talyllyn Railway station. On the right is the engine *Cambrai* and *Dolgoch* is standing on the left, having arrived with our train from Abergynolwyn. The sea is in the distance and the fashions of the day – mainly zippers and slacks or jeans – don't look too out of date.

Talyllyn Railway No. 1 *Talyllyn* was a mere ninety-five years young when photographed at Towyn Wharf in September 1960. (Ron Fisher)

On 22 August 1966, Talyllyn Railway No. 4 *Edward Thomas* is being serviced at Towyn Wharf. Note the huge Giesl Oblong Ejector with which this engine was fitted during the 1960s. This was later removed. The buffers on the Talyllyn are unusual on narrow gauge engines.

The Talyllyn Railway's Fletcher Jennings tank engine *Dolgoch* is seen here at Abergynolwyn on 22 August 1966 in the green livery that suits it so well.

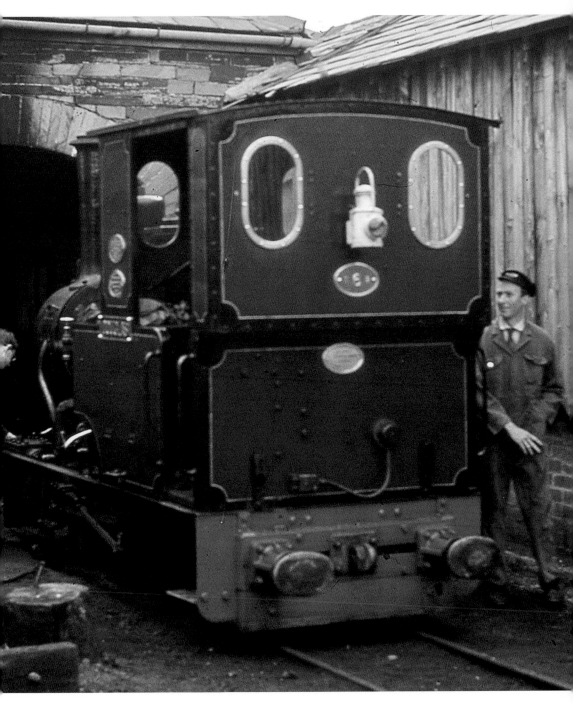

Standing outside the shed at Towyn Pendre is Barclay 0-4-0T No. 6 *Douglas* painted in the Talyllyn Railway's very attractive lined green livery. At the time this was the newest addition to the fleet.

Here we get a good view of the rolling stock of our train, which has arrived at Abergynolwyn, the end of the line, on 22 August 1966. Nearest the camera is the ex-Corris coach, beautifully rebuilt, while a Glyn Valley Tramway vehicle can be seen further on. This is a fair load for little old *Dolgoch*.

At Brynglas in 1966 our train passes an eastbound service headed by 0-4-2ST No. 4 *Edward Thomas* and tokens are exchanged. Note the very well-engineered track and the rolling countryside.

Dolgoch in August 1968 at Towyn Wharf departing on a lovely summer's day, watched by a group of admirers, with the splendid Corris coach fully loaded. (Bryan Jeyes)

0-4-2T No. 1 *Talyllyn* at Towyn Wharf is waiting to leave with a train for Abergynolwyn on 13 August 1967. The platforms look almost deserted, yet it was a Monday in peak holiday season. (Bryan Jeyes)

Douglas takes water at Dolgoch – sadly the old stone water tower had at this time (August 1967) been taken out of use.

In August 1968, *Talyllyn* is on the bridge at Dolgoch amid high summer foliage. Delightful scenes like this give the railway its unique character. (Bryan Jeyes)

A panoramic view of Towyn, which reveals the close proximity of the Cambrian main line. The siding adjacent to Towyn Wharf station was often used to offload items brought by BR. *Edward Thomas* is in the station. (Bryan Jeyes)

A feature of both the Festiniog and Talyllyn Railways in the 1960s was the costumed Welsh lady – here seen at Towyn Wharf on 14 August 1966.

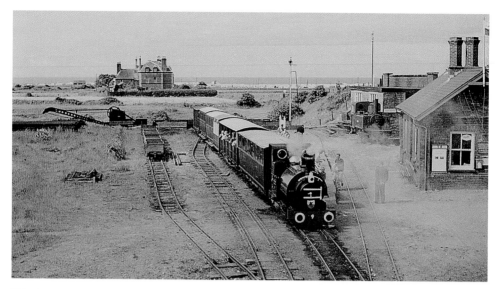

Talyllyn Railway 0-4-2T No. 1 *Talyllyn* waits to depart from Towyn Wharf in June 1961 with a train to Abergynolwyn. In the background can be seen *Cambrai*, a metre-gauge 0-6-0T that worked in France until 1936, when it was bought by the Loddington Ironstone Company near Kettering in Northamptonshire. It is now at the Narrow Gauge Railway Museum at Irchester, near Wellingborough. (Ron Fisher)

Ex-Corris Railway Kerr Stuart 0-4-2ST No.4 *Edward Thomas* is seen at the Brynglas passing loop in September 1960. (Ron Fisher)

The Fairbourne Railway

Arriving at the Fairbourne Railway on a warm summer evening to catch the last train of the day proved something of a shock. My knowledge of this 2-mile-long line was very limited. To step into the station and see a big and impressive 2-4-2 tender engine standing at the head of the train was a pleasant surprise. The engine bore the name *Katie* and her green paintwork was offset by polished brass and a gleaming red buffer beam. There was more than a whiff of Great Western about her. We stepped aboard the open coach and soon *Katie* was off, nonchalantly hauling her almost empty train on a very pleasant ride alongside the sand dunes that protected the railway from the sea.

Miniature railways fall into two camps: the serious ones like the Romney, Hythe & Dymchurch, and the fun ones enclosed within parks or other attractions. The Fairbourne struck me as very definitely in category one. Not only that, but it had a great sense of purpose. We eventually arrived at Ferry station, a lonely platform surrounded by shingle, with a flag flying bravely in the evening breeze. People strolled along the coastline as *Katie* ran round her train and we took in the mountain scenery and views of the setting sun. Yet, enjoyable though this was, the Fairbourne was actually built with more serious intent – to transport passengers to catch the ferry across the bay to Barmouth. I took several trips on the line, being hauled by *Katie*, her sister *Siân* and a happy little diesel called *Rachel*. Boyd, in his history of the line, says the rails never exceed 15 feet above sea level! Certainly it looks as if a fierce storm might wash the whole thing away. Equally precarious is the Fairbourne's history. Built as a 2-foot gauge railway in 1895, it was converted to 15-inch gauge in 1916, and after some tricky years between the wars, had to be resuscitated by a group of Midland businessmen in 1946. The railway says its heyday was in the 1960s and 1970s, but due partly to competition from other narrow gauge lines, business fell away and in 1984 it changed ownership once more and was altered to 12¼-inch gauge. In the 1990s it was for sale yet again and fell into disrepair, but Lady Luck smiled and it was rescued for the fourth time. Now it is in the hands of a charitable trust.

All this means that the 1960s were a great time to visit the Fairbourne. If you are in west Wales, don't miss the chance to take a trip, as it has an honourable place as one of the Great Little Trains of Wales. I am sure the old ferry boat *Stingray* seen in my picture has long passed into history, but I think a day on the Fairbourne is time well spent.

Rachel stands at Fairbourne on the evening of 22 August 1966. This engine is still at work, now based at a country park in Wigan.

Among all the historic narrow gauge lines in Wales, the Fairbourne Railway has a tendency to get a bit overlooked, but you can see from this picture that it really was quite an impressive operation. Here the driver of *Katie*, an attractive 2-4-2 built in 1954, prepares to take the last train of the day to Ferry Point on 22 August 1966. (Bryan Jeyes)

The impressive front end of *Katie* at Fairbourne on 22 August 1966. Despite officially being a 'miniature' railway, the beefy engines and 2 miles of track elevate it to the bigger league.

At the end of the line on the Fairbourne Railway there were just one or two passengers for the last trip of the day. This is Ferry Point, where you could catch the ferry to Barmouth. As you can see, this station is right on the beach. There is a definite hint of Great Western about the design of *Katie*. (Bryan Jeyes)

The sun goes down behind *Katie* at Ferry Point in August 1966 – a unique setting on the Welsh narrow gauge. (Bryan Jeyes)

The Fairbourne Railway runs along the sand at this coastal town. Seen at Golf Links Halt, an early morning service is powered by diesel locomotive *Rachel* on 26 August 1966.

The main engines at the Fairbourne Railway in 1966 were two impressive-looking 2-4-2 steam locomotives, *Katie* and *Siân*. Here we see *Katie* running tender first on 26 August 1966 with a very light train.

The little ferry boat *Stingray* is seen at Ferry Point having just brought a load of passengers across from Barmouth. It appears a very rudimentary way of crossing the bay but the captain certainly looks professional. From here you took the Fairbourne Railway along the sands and still can, as the service operates today (in a modern boat) when the trains are running. 8 August 1967.

Taken on 14 August 1967, this picture gives a good general view of the Fairbourne Railway's Ferry Point station. We never actually caught the ferry to Barmouth, just used the train for a pleasant ride.

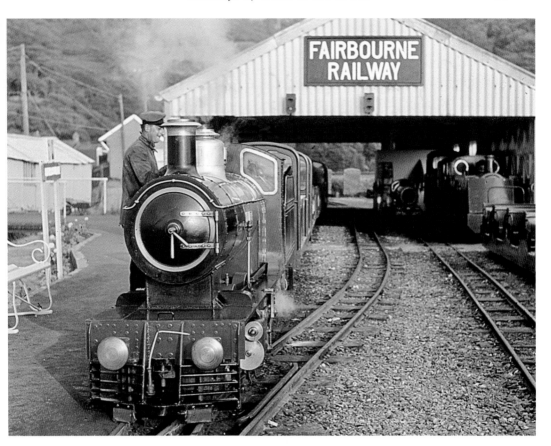

Fairbourne station was a miniature version of a main line terminus. Here, *Katie* waits to work a train while sister *Siân* is tucked away in her shed in August 1966. These engines survive today, but not at the Fairbourne.

The Festiniog Railway

The prolific writer on light railways W. J. K. Davies summed up the Festiniog Railway like this: 'It was,' he said, 'the first to show that the narrow gauge could be taken really seriously as a means of transport.' It didn't seem that way back in the 1960s. The line ran only 7 miles to Tan-y-Bwlch, half its original length. The idea of re-opening the complete railway plus the abandoned Welsh Highland as well seemed incredulous. Yet there was no doubt that something tangible separated the Festiniog from its neighbours. Was it the formidable double-ended Fairlie locomotives? Or maybe the society magazine with its ambitious talk of electrification and colour light signals? Or perhaps it was Boston Lodge Works, a vast labyrinth of workshops and storerooms and yards, where complete locomotives could actually be constructed? Maybe it was a combination of these things; certainly nothing like this existed elsewhere on the narrow gauge in these islands. Even in its 1960s contracted state, the Festiniog was personified with an impressive air of self-importance, a dynastic entity energetically recovering from a spell in intensive care. Built in 1836 as a horse-worked line to move slate from quarries up around Blaenau Ffestiniog, initially trains headed downhill by gravity. The problem was a couple of uphill sections, which at first prohibited this, so the 730-yard-long and very narrow Moelwyn Tunnel was drilled through the mountains above Tan-y-Bwlch. In 1863 narrow gauge steam locomotives were introduced and only seven years later the first Fairlie arrived. Truly this was an inventive and pioneering operation, which remained prosperous until the 1920s when slate traffic declined and everything was patched up to keep it going. Then came a disastrous lease of the hugely unprofitable Welsh Highland Railway. By 1946 it was all over.

Except, of course, it wasn't. Buoyed by the success of the enthusiast-run Talyllyn Railway, a bunch of guys, some of whom had been involved with the Talyllyn, revived the dormant Festiniog, getting the engine *Prince* back in steam. Two Fairlies followed, and then two locomotives were acquired from the Penrhyn Quarry, *Linda* and *Blanche*, which today seem so much part of the Festiniog Railway that they might as well have been built at Boston Lodge.

Back in the 1960s, the line was run by ex-BR manager Allan Garraway, who had been a key figure in reviving the line in 1955. He managed to combine his operational tasks with regular spells at the regulator of *Linda* and you can see him at work in a couple of my photographs. Unlike most enthusiasts of the time, we enjoyed *all* of the Festiniog – that means the closed section as well. Part of the line above Dduallt had been covered by a new Central Electricity Generating Board reservoir (they dismissed the Festiniog's protests as 'amateurs playing with trains'). This flooded the north end of the Moelwyn Tunnel, but we walked a long way into the cold, damp artery one day from the south and also explored much of the old line near Blaenau.

The Festiniog of the 1960s had all the charm of a typical Welsh narrow gauge line, with antique locomotives and coaches, but elevated to the next level. Happily the electrification idea was soon forgotten as an aberration, but the Festiniog is still the greatest narrow gauge ride in the UK and was so in the 1960s. The first part sees trains leaving Harbour station, back then a fairly rudimentary operation, and striding out across the Cob, a man-made embankment over the sea, before swinging left past Boston Lodge Works and climbing into the hills. The idea that you might one day be able to travel back to Blaenau never occurred to us, but we now know it was very much in the minds of Garraway and his team.

With their dark green paint and green and cream coaches (with red ends), the trains looked a picture. They were impressive rather than handsome, but you always had the feeling you were going to get there. In the early 1970s I had the chance to make a return trip to Dduallt in the cab of *Blanche*. It was an amazing experience as everything alongside the train seemed so close. Today the railway has a huge fleet of engines and 38 miles of track (including the Welsh Highland) and is in another league. But I think it always was.

Drifting downhill, Fairlie 0-4-4-0T *Merddin Emrys* crosses Cei Mawr embankment in April 1962, shortly after being restored to service, and is running painted in primer. (Ron Fisher)

Resplendent in a fresh coat of green is double Fairlie 0-4-4-0T *Merddin Emrys*. Tube cleaning is in progress in the Works Yard at Boston Lodge on 21 April 1963. It ran for a while in this roofless, rather naked state after restoration. (Ron Fisher)

In June 1964 ex-Penrhyn Quarry Railway 0-4-0ST *Linda* rounds Boston Lodge curve with another train for Tan-y-Bwlch. The Festiniog Railway's General Manager, Allan Garraway, is in charge. Note the vintage caravan on the road below. (Ron Fisher)

Top Link A4 Pacific driver Bill Hoole spent his retirement driving narrow gauge trains on the Festiniog Railway. He is seen here shovelling coal from wagon No. 60 into the tender of *Prince* at Boston Lodge Works in June 1964. Repeated washing by his wife Dolly had turned his dark blue overalls into the pale colour shown here. (Ron Fisher)

An overall view of the Festiniog Railway's upper terminus at Tan-y-Bwlch in June 1964. *Linda* has run round her train and is ready to set off back to Porthmadog. Tan-y-Bwlch is still a favourite stopping off point for many of the Festiniog Railway's passengers as it is the starting point for many delightful walks. (Ron Fisher)

A relief Annual General Meeting day special train was run on 20 April 1963. It is seen here just above Penrhyn Crossing behind *Prince*. (Ron Fisher)

A working party in February 1963 on the Festiniog Railway is blessed with glorious sunshine following weeks of snow. This is the scene at Milestone curve, showing the Wickham Trolley, which was the Permanent Way Department's transport at the time. (Ron Fisher)

Welsh Pony, one of the larger George England engines, was exhibited in Birmingham in 1963 and is seen here after its return. Looking rather forlorn, it stands in Glan-y-Mor yard at Boston Lodge Works on 21 April of that year. (Ron Fisher)

Prince was 100 years old in 1963. It is seen here descending Gwyndy Bank towards Minffordd under a cloudless blue sky in June of that year. The ex-Lynton & Barnstaple Railway coach, now Festiniog Railway buffet car No. 14, is clearly bigger than the adjoining observation car. (Ron Fisher)

This very attractive scene shows the harbour at Portmadoc on 23 August 1966, a wonderful hot day with the last vestiges of cloud dissipating.

A general view of Tan-y-Bwlch station on 25 August 1966. Waiting to head a train back to Porthmadog is the ex-Penrhyn 0-4-0ST *Blanche*. Those Wall's ice cream signs could be seen everywhere in Britain at the time.

Beyond hope – *Palmerston* is seen here at Glan-y-Mor on 25 August 1966. This was the original 0-4-0ST in the worst condition – just look at the cab roof. Yet miracles are possible and it has been running again for quite some time.

Double Fairlie locomotive No. 3 *Earl of Merioneth* is under overhaul at Boston Lodge Works on 25 August 1966, giving a good view of the unique boilers fitted to this type of engine. The firehole doors are on the other side. (Bryan Jeyes)

A closer view of the ex-Penrhyn 0-4-0ST *Blanche* at Tan-y-Bwlch in 1966 shows her huge and rather ugly tender cab, which rather spoils the proportions of this engine. Some years later I had a ride in the cab of this engine up the line to Dduallt and it was a wonderful experience.

The main train of the day, *Y Cymro* is getting away from Porthmadog behind the 0-4-0 locomotive *Blanche*. It was probably quite a tough job for this modest locomotive. The weird but useful Simplex diesel is on the left.

The narrow gauge tracks lead enticingly towards the Moelwyn Tunnel, but there will be no trains here today as the tunnel is blocked forever at the other end. This shows the superb scenery traversed by the Festiniog Railway and the challenge faced in getting back to Blaenau Ffestiniog.

Here we see the abandoned stretch of the Festiniog Railway above Dduallt on its way to Moelwyn Tunnel in August 1966. The track actually looks in pretty decent shape. Note the very rudimentary bridge and dry stone walls very close to the track.

On 23 August 1966 the ex-Penrhyn Quarry saddle tank *Linda* passes over Penrhyn Crossing and we get a good view of the crew at work.

Here we have travelled up from Porthmadog on 25 August 1966 and *Blanche* is seen at Tan-y-Bwlch, a very attractive setting.

This is a classic view of the Festiniog Railway in the 1960s. Double Fairlie No. 3 *Earl of Merioneth* is setting out across the Cob on a pleasant summer's day, 18 August 1967. Behind her is a very mixed rake of stock, including the 'bug boxes', which were then 100 years old and good fun to ride in. Harbour station is in the distance.

The crew of Festiniog Railway 0-4-0T *Linda* prepare their locomotive for the climb towards Tan-y-Bwlch on 20 August 1967. The low tender gives a good view of the controls and both gauge glasses look nicely full. Allan Garraway is again the driver.

A slightly unusual view from above taken in 1967 at Tan-y-Bwlch. The 0-4-0ST *Linda* is about to return to Porthmadog with her train, running tender first and a bit short of coal. The crew are deep in conversation.

In August 1967, *Earl of Merioneth* is tackling Whistling Curve as the Fairlie climbs powerfully through the Welsh hills. (Bryan Jeyes)

Prince is seen here at Porthmadog in July 1967 in a strangely peaceful picture, considering it was high season. We get a wonderful view across the Cob as the little engine reverses into Harbour station. Compare this with today's scene! (Bryan Jeyes)

Blanche crosses the Cob in 1966 with a train of more modern stock. The teak-look coaches seem less attractive than the previous green and cream.

High up on the last stretch towards Tan-y-Bwlch is *Linda*, which is working very hard without emitting much visible evidence on a sultry summer day in August 1966.

Prince and the Festiniog Railway are inseparable. Here on 18 August 1967 we see her gleaming at Boston Lodge. In those days you could just wander round the works and always got a friendly welcome.

Two old Ford cars from the 1950s stand either side of the abandoned route at Tanygrisiau, not far from Blaenau, seen here on a misty August day in 1966. On returning (by train) fifty years later there was nothing I could recognise.

Blaenau Ffestiniog in August 1966, with narrow gauge tracks still in place. Across the wall on the right was the BR station. The dramatic backdrop is evident in this view looking towards Porthmadog.

Linda at Minffordd in August 1967, passing the sign pointing to the BR station. Road and rails are alongside each other at this point. (Bryan Jeyes)

Minffordd's elegant Festiniog Railway station, seen here in October 1965, dwarfs the nearby GWR building. (Bryan Jeyes)

Moelwyn had been part of the Festiniog fleet for forty years when photographed with a coal train at Minffordd in October 1965. Its peculiar looks result from being American-made and then rebuilt with very odd front carrier wheels to improve its riding. (Bryan Jeyes)

Another Festiniog oddity in 1966 was this newly arrived 0-4-0 + 0-4-0 Garratt, the first one ever built. It would have been fun to see it squeezing through the Garnedd Tunnel, but after many years on the sidelines it found a home working the other way out of Porthmadog – on the Welsh Highland.

Moelwyn outside Boston Lodge Works in August 1967, with a beefy headlight and jaunty vacuum pipe. She was kept at the ready in case of failures, being quite capable of passenger work if needed. Her appearance has changed somewhat over the years.

Prince and *Blanche* outside Boston Lodge in 1967, being prepared for the day's work.

It is worth comparing this view with that of today as *Linda* sets off across the Cob. We can see straight ahead along the road where the Welsh Highland now runs.

Looking towards the joint Great Western/Festiniog Railway station in the centre of Blaenau Ffestiniog, we can see the link through to the LNWR exchange sidings on the left, with the North Western Hotel behind the wall, in June 1962. (Ron Fisher)

The massive Oakley Quarry dominates this view of Blaenau Ffestiniog, but the site of the Festiniog Railway's old Stesion Fein can be clearly seen opposite the BR (ex-LNWR) station. The water tank is still in existence and there are wagons in the BR goods yard in June 1962. (Ron Fisher)

We leave the Festiniog with a classic scene captured by Bryan Jeyes – *Prince* setting off across the Cob with a wedding train on a sunny day in October 1965. The four coaches include old No. 12, built in 1880 as a luggage van and seen here in use as a buffet car. (Bryan Jeyes)

The Vale of Rheidol Light Railway

We liked the Vale of Rheidol for lots of reasons, but mainly because it was professional. A paid crew ran trains to try to make some money for the ailing enterprise that was British Railways, and in lots of ways it was the big railway made smaller. That didn't mean they cared any less about giving the punters a good time, but their motivation was different. You could see this everywhere. The engines were sort of cleaned, and got grubbier as the 1960s progressed. This gave them an attractive workaday look. Coal was strewn in front of the safety valve as there was no bunker. The number and nameplates were huge and were always kept polished. The three engines were painted in BR colours, in itself very attractive, but a few years later they appeared looking absurd in diesel blue. What a brilliant demonstration of corporatism gone crazy!

You could photograph a locomotive at the narrow gauge station in Aberystwyth, with a full-size train behind it in the main station. All good fun. The 'all aboard' and wave of the green flag could just as easily be sending the 'Cambrian Coast Express' on its way to Paddington. Both driver and fireman were wearing BR jackets and grubby grease top caps – just standard BR steam apparel. Once the engine was moving, it became clear that this railway was special. All the action took place on the left-hand side as you climbed up the valley on a trackbed as sturdy as the 2-6-2 tank locomotives that used it. It was actually quite a new creation, being opened in 1902 to provide transport for timber, the lead mines in the district and tourists. The goods traffic only lasted twenty years, but the line prospered as a delightful way to reach the Rheidol Falls. You have to give the Great Western Railway credit: they kept the line in fine condition, building new coaches to exploit the views and sending the engines to Swindon when they needed overhauls. British Railways kept up the momentum in the 1960s without ever getting too excited about their only remaining narrow gauge line. When privatised in 1989, it had survived for more than twenty years as BR's only steam-hauled line.

A 1961 advertisement encouraged visitors to 'See the Rheidol Valley, a journey through 12 miles of magnificent scenery for a fare of 6/- return'. Well, that's 30p today, so it hardly broke the bank. At Devil's Bridge, you could enjoy the falls and have a cup of tea and a cake for a total of 6d (2½p). The station was painted brown and cream in Great Western style and was a bit rudimentary, but the signals were big and businesslike, like those on the Welshpool line. Today the station has been beautified and the track work looks immaculate. Trains now run from the main station at Aberystwyth, and if a spot of oil should accidentally fall on the pristine paintwork of any of the three locomotives, it will be immediately wiped away, so it is receiving the love and care it never quite had in the 1960s. Even so, I'm rather glad that I saw it when it was just that little bit scruffy.

Here we see No. 9 *Prince of Wales* being prepared for the day's run up to Rheidol Falls on 16 August 1967. The cleaner is making sure the side tanks and nameplate are clean, but that's about it.

We're at Aberystwyth and No. 8 *Llywelyn* has uncoupled and is heading for the loco shed on 24 August 1966.

Now we are well into the climb up the Rheidol Valley in August 1966 and you can see the ledge on the left hillside that marks the path of the train.

Prince of Wales has reached Devil's Bridge and is being watered and serviced prior to a siesta before returning to Aberystwyth on 16 April 1967.

This is quite a timeless view at Devil's Bridge, with locomotive No. 8 *Llywelyn* waiting to leave for Aberystwyth in 1966. I like the Great Western feel of this picture.

Llywelyn is at Devil's Bridge on 24 August 1966, having arrived from Aberystwyth. I really enjoyed this trip on a beautiful day.

A newly repainted sign at Devil's Bridge station on 24 August 1966. I like the reversed letter 'N'. A cup of tea was 3*d*!

Prince of Wales, whose name has been copied for the new LNER P2 2-8-2 that is to be built. What a peculiar name to attach to a class of engine so strongly associated with Scotland, unlike this one, which has spent all its life in the Welsh hills. No. 9 has coupled up at Devil's Bridge for the return journey, which is basically all downhill.

It is now August 1968 and *Prince of Wales* has received a much-needed repaint, plus a new smokebox numberplate. The blue livery sits uncomfortably on this engine. (Bryan Jeyes)

Vale of Rheidol Railway No. 9 *Prince of Wales* crosses a minor road with an ungated level crossing on its way down to Aberystwyth with a train from Devil's Bridge in June 1964. (Ron Fisher)

Vale of Rheidol Railway 2-6-2T No. 8 *Llywelyn* takes water at Aberffrwd on its way from Aberystwyth up to Devil's Bridge with a Gainsborough Model Railway Society special train in June 1964. (Ron Fisher)

No. 8 has backed onto her train and is waiting for passengers to climb aboard at Aberystwyth narrow gauge station on 24 August 1966. Today these trains use the main station. Note the oil can perched near the chimney.

The Snowdon Mountain Railway

When you stand at the bottom of a mountain on a clear day and look upwards, is the first thing that enters your mind, 'I reckon it would be good to build a railway up there?' Possibly not. But then you are not Sir Richard Moon, chairman of the London & North Western Railway. He was peering up Snowdon and he had an idea. Long and acrimonious debates involving local landowners then continued from the time of Sir Richard's vision in 1869 until the start of construction twenty-five years later. As the company had acquired all the land they needed, the fuss and bother of an Act of Parliament was unnecessary. On its website, the railway neatly recalls that Sir Richard lived in 'the age of the destination', and where better than a thousand metres high in the mountains of North Wales?

The redoubtable Victorian engineers were called upon to exercise all their construction skills and decided on a rack system, which meant the locomotive's cylinders turned two geared cog wheels that rotated in a rack and propelled the engine uphill. It had the extra advantage of offering braking when descending. The idea was already in use in Switzerland and it worked. It wasn't all plain sailing, however. On the opening day No. 1 *Ladas* derailed and was destroyed when the engine's cogs jumped out of the rack and it plunged into a ravine. Guard rails enclosing the rack and lighter coaches solved this problem and the line has had an impressive safety record ever since.

In 1966 we arrived at Llanberis eager to travel, but were frightened away by the queue and the ticket prices. The following year we were prepared with extra cash – there were no 'live now, pay later' credit cards in the 1960s. As well as a bulging wallet, the Snowdon Mountain Railway demands good weather. On misty days trains will not get to the summit and obviously it doesn't run in high winds. Luckily the weather was perfect for our journey. The experience is unlike any other narrow gauge railway and exactly like any other rack railway. The engine pushes its single coach and after leaving Llanberis on the level the train immediately starts a relentless climb. Passing another train which is descending is an odd experience. But our locomotive, No. 7 *Ralph*, was entirely at home, coping with the amazing gradient and the sinking temperature as we reached Summit station. If you are not feeling energetic, you can watch the climbers with thankful relief and enjoy the fact that someone, or at least something else, is doing the hard work.

These days you can travel with what they call a 'traditional' diesel, but I think that would spoil the fun, even if these services are a bit cheaper and much more frequent. Besides, the 'traditional' engine is surely steam? Once at the top, the views are fantastic, and while we may not have the vision of Sir Richard Moon, we can certainly offer a word of thanks to him when gazing across the rugged skyline.

A Snowdon Mountain Railway train is moving out of Llanberis on 23 August 1966. The engine is No. 6 *Padarn.*

No 7. *Ralph* is prepared for service at Llanberis on 15 August 1967, another location where you could just wander around the shed and receive a warm welcome.

We are cautiously descending from Snowdon on 15 August 1967 and you can see the rack rail on the left. These days I gather many trains are diesel-hauled, which would not be the same thing at all. You definitely need steam for this trip if you are an enthusiast.

Climbers gather to watch another train pass by on this spectacular railway in August 1968. (Bryan Jeyes)

The Corris Railway

The Corris Railway, like its near neighbour the Talyllyn, was a 2-foot 3-inch gauge slate carrier that opened in 1859. Steam power arrived in 1878 in the shape of three very attractive little 0-4-0 saddle tank engines, each later converted to 0-4-2 by the addition of a pair of skateboard-sized trailing wheels. Services ran from a station adjacent to the main line buildings at Machynlleth to Aberllefenni, linking up with various quarries. Passenger trains were discontinued in 1931, and by that time the Corris was owned – a bit reluctantly – by the Great Western Railway. It was nationalised in 1948 and in that year floods damaged the line at the bridge across the River Dyfi near Machynlleth. Some debate exists over whether this was the factor that led to its complete closure, or whether British Railways simply saw no future for it. In August 1948 the last train ran, and the two remaining engines were sold to the Talyllyn Railway.

We explored parts of this old line in the 1960s and followed its route from Machynlleth northwards, but there wasn't too much to see. However, one thing we know about Welsh narrow gauge railways is that there is likely to be someone out there with the Big Plan. Today the Corris is being cautiously revived from its old sheds at Maespoeth and they have ambitions to head south towards Machynlleth.

In August 1966 we see the old Corris Railway terminus station at Machynlleth. It was in pretty good condition considering the line had been closed for nearly twenty years. The Cambrian line station, with similar architecture, is on the left.

The first station out of Machynlleth was Fridd Gate, the site of which was right by the road heading north out of the town. It seen here in August 1966.

The Welsh Highland Railway

We couldn't resist the chance to explore some of the old Welsh Highland, having read its tortuous history. When it closed in 1936, its legal status was a mess. The Festiniog surrendered its lease (very thankfully, I should imagine). The rails were lifted in 1941, but the route of the line remained pretty much undisturbed. We did some walks along the sturdy trackbed, some of it still with ballast in place, admiring the spectacular scenery. At Beddgelert, a new organisation called the Welsh Highland Light Railway (1964) Ltd had started assembling items to re-open a section of it. This eventually happened, but it was the mighty Ffestiniog Railway that actually recreated the full Welsh Highland after lengthy legal shenanigans. Even in its rebirth, the Welsh Highland was not easy. Well, maybe in the 1960s it actually was *easier*, because it was in limbo and the few pictures I took will one day seem just a peculiar interlude during the time when the Welsh Highland was temporarily dormant.

Ron Fisher walked the whole of the Welsh Highland back in 1960. It must have been a wonderful experience. Here is Tryfan Junction station on 16 April of that year, which now sees trains passing once again. (Ron Fisher)

Even though the restoration of the Welsh Highland Railway was many years away, an embryonic organisation had been set up in 1964 to revive part of the line, based on the old station at Beddgelert. We made a visit on our way back from Snowdon on 23 August 1966 and you can see their tentative first efforts to assemble stock.

Beddgelert Tunnel on 23 August 1966. We were already interested in this old line running through spectacular scenery. Once again the trackbed is in good condition.

Nantmor on the old Welsh Highland Railway on 15 August 1967 with the trackbed looking in remarkably good condition.

The Welsh Highland's route was quite complicated around Beddgelert and there were one or two short sections of infrastructure that were never used. This is one of them on 23 August 1966.

We also visited the old Glyn Valley Tramway station at Glyn Ceiriog as seen in August 1966. Efforts are being made to build a new Glyn Valley Tramway, but getting to use this building, Glyn Ceiriog station, will again be a challenge.

The North Wales Coast Line

The most important lines in Wales ran along the north and south coasts. We'll leave the fascinating array of valleys and main lines in the south for another time. One day we set off for Llandudno Junction; note that we did not go to the resort of Llandudno, as we had no intention of getting our feet wet. The Junction station was much more interesting, with trains on summer Saturdays passing through every few minutes. The line runs from Crewe and Chester to Conway and then over the Britannia Bridge, eventually ending up at Holyhead. Those who remember the names of the Patriot Class 4-6-0s will know the many other places it served – Rhyl, Prestatyn, Colwyn Bay and others. Our visit in the 1960s started with a glimpse of a 'Jubilee' 4-6-0 standing in the station just where we couldn't quite photograph it properly. It then pulled out. As there were very few Jubilees still at work, this was a bad start. Happily, it only went up the branch to Llandudno and then returned to the shed at Llandudno Junction for servicing.

There was a constant stream of trains passing through, hauled mainly by Class 5s. We saw virtually no diesels. The freights included one pulled by an immaculate 8F 2-8-0, No. 48151. You may recognise this as the preserved 8F run today by the West Coast Railway Company. I can assure you it was every bit as immaculate when it stopped for a crew change at Llandudno Junction in 1966, having just been through the works for a major overhaul. A few years earlier and the variety of engines would have been greater. Holyhead had a stud of 'Britannias' to work its Euston services and the odd Stanier Pacific made a foray along the North Wales Coast line after they were displaced from the most important West Coast route services. A year ago I was back at Llandudno Junction and it was still busy. I have also been to Holyhead behind *Princess Elizabeth* on a steam special. Llandudno Junction is never going to be one of the spectacular stations of Wales, but it does bring back happy memories of what an all-steam summer Saturday was like.

A Crewe South-based Stanier Class 5, No. 44836, waits at Llandudno Junction on 27 August 1966 after arriving from the east. (Bryan Jeyes)

Now preserved, 8F No. 48151 is seen here on a short train of tank wagons from Amlwch to Ellesmere Port at Llandudno Junction on 27 August 1966. (Bryan Jeyes)

Jubilee No. 45647 *Sturdee* is running through Llandudno Junction station on 27 August 1966, having worked the 09.15 from Leeds to Llandudno. Having arrived tender first, she is now crossing to the south of the station to gain access to the shed. Cleaning the tender is clearly a work in progress. (Bryan Jeyes)

Famous for its name if nothing else, Llanfairpwllgwyngyllgogerychwyrndrobwllllantysiliogogogoch is the first station on Ynys Mon (Anglesey). Closed in 1966, it reopened between 1970 and 1974, when it closed again before being reopened once more in 1993. This view was taken in June 1961. (Ron Fisher)

Blaenau Ffestiniog LNWR station, seen here in June 1962, is at the end of a long branch from Llandudno Junction. The car is a 1949 Hillman Minx. (Ron Fisher)

On 12 April 1963, we are on a train that has passed through the Conway Tubular Bridge and is running under the towering battlements of Conway Castle. (Ron Fisher)

A passenger train running into Llandudno Junction from the west on 27 August 1966 is headed by Class 5 4-6-0 No. 45283.

Ivatt 2-6-2 tanks Nos 41200 and 41234 have just arrived at Llanberis from Caernarfon with the Stephenson Locomotive Society/Manchester Locomotive Society Caernarvonshire Railtour on 20 October 1963. (Ron Fisher)

Llanberis station, having been closed for three years, is in excellent condition in 1966 and actually looks to have been recently repainted.

The Ruabon to Barmouth Line

Three railways ran east to west across mid- and north Wales in the early 1960s. By 1966 there were only two. The casualty was the Great Western route from Ruabon to Barmouth, which ran through Llangollen and Bala on its way to the seaside. At Barmouth Junction – later Morfa Mawddach – it joined the Cambrian main line and crossed the long bridge over the River Dovey to reach the holiday resort of Barmouth. Early in 1965 the line had been served with an execution warrant by Dr Beeching and by the end of the 1960s the track had gone and trains meandering through the rolling hills were but a memory. The line had plenty of steep gradients, charming Great Western stations that clearly had not changed in decades and a bunch of energetic locomotives, mainly smaller Great Western types and some BR Standards.

Intrepid as ever, we decided that this line was worth exploring, so we set out one afternoon to visit as many stations as possible. We finished when it got dark. The line in those days was still in excellent condition and the 30 miles or so we visited gave a great sense of the superb countryside witnessed by those fortunate enough to see it from a carriage window. It was a single track with passing places and felt very Great Western. Maybe wandering around a closed station set in lovely scenery is not everyone's idea of an absorbing way to spend a holiday, but for me it was just about perfect and I shall not easily forget standing on the abandoned platforms at Drws-y-Nant in the warm evening sunshine and imagining a Class 4300 2-6-0 approaching from Barmouth with three coaches, ready to restart on the challenging 1 in 64 gradient. The rails were rusty and a bit weedy, but otherwise everything was ready for a couple of passengers to appear, taking in the tree-covered hills before boarding the short train and setting off for who knows where.

Features of these stations included huge name boards, corrugated iron waiting shelters, tall spiralling chimneys on the station buildings and the inevitable row of telegraph poles leading off into the distance. I can get a bit misty-eyed about such scenes but, let's be honest, it was the railway at its enchanting best, blending happily into the environment in a way that a modern bus shelter never can. Study the pictures and see if you share these emotions.

The final station we visited was Bala (New), which was the first stop on the branch from Bala Junction to Blaenau Ffestiniog. This station replaced an earlier Bala station on the Ruabon–Barmouth line and looked very similar to those on that railway. It remained open after the rest of the route to Blaenau closed in 1961, offering a connection to Bala Junction, but closed with the Ruabon line in 1965. There was a most impressive goods shed here, with turrets and battlements, having been built to resemble a castle to appease a local landowner.

Most of the stations we saw have been swept away, although some platforms remain. A new narrow gauge line, the Bala Lake Railway, has been constructed along part of the route. The eastern end of the line has been re-opened as a standard gauge heritage line from Llangollen to Corwen. This is great news, but it's not the same.

Stand in the middle of a field at Garneddwen Halt and survey your surroundings. Watch a 2-6-0 locomotive approach the tiny platforms, pause, and then set off towards the coast. It's a cocktail that beats a craft gin and tonic!

Arthog, seen here in August 1966, was the first station east of Barmouth Junction, a fairly unprepossessing halt with wooden platforms. The trackbed is now a footpath, but the station has disappeared.

Dolgellau station had extensive sidings and a turntable, but was demolished to make way for road improvements in the 1970s.

Bontnewydd was the first station east of Dolgellau on the line to Ruabon, photographed in August 1966. This was a very attractive railway and it's so sad that it was closed.

Set amid superb scenery, Drws-y-Nant station, seen here in 1966, was swept away by a road improvement scheme.

This tiny station, Garneddwen Halt, was on the Ruabon–Barmouth line, which closed in 1965. We drove east, photographing stations on this route, on 23 August 1966, when everything was still intact. Westbound freights were often banked to this point from Llanuwchllyn.

Llanuwchllyn was another very attractive station on the Ruabon–Barmouth line, but the scenery is not quite as good as the stations situated to the west. You can see the rails converging to a single track and appearing to head uphill. This is now part of the Bala Lake Railway. (Bryan Jeyes)

Bala (New) was the first station on the old line to Blaenau Ffestiniog from Bala Junction on the Great Western Ruabon–Barmouth line. The route had been closed the year before I photographed it on 23 August 1966. A fire station now occupies this site.

This wonderful goods shed, with turrets, was pictured at Bala station on the evening of 23 August 1966. A local landowner objected to the building of the line, so this ornate goods shed was built to appease him. Maybe he thought it looked like Harlech Castle!

The Cambrian Coast Line

Imagine building a station that virtually no-one can access, except by train. The Cambrian Railways were not alone in this. Berney Arms in Norfolk comes to mind, approached from your boat (seriously) by a path across a field, and it's still open after 170 years. Salcey Forest in Northamptonshire was reached by a remote, long track across pastures. Obviously no-one used it, so it closed after four months. Dovey Junction has done rather better, opening in the 1860s and still going strong today. It is situated at the point where trains, having wearily worked their way across Wales from Shrewsbury, head either south along the coast to Aberystwyth or north along the coast to Barmouth and Pwllheli. In steam days, the two portions of the Cambrian Coast Express – one from each direction – would link up here and head for Shrewsbury and Paddington. The joined up train would then arrive at Machynlleth, bustling with importance, before setting off across the hills eastwards. The driver would be hoping for a good engine – this was hard work for a modest Class 4 locomotive. Once the express had departed, the signals would clear for another arrival from Dovey

Junction. This would be the light engine that had pulled the Pwllheli portion and was now heading for the shed at Machynlleth to await servicing and a return trip to Pwllheli later that day.

Two locomotives dominated the Cambrian Coast Express during our first holiday: 4-6-0 No. 75016 on the main train from Aberystwyth and 2-6-0 No. 76040 on the Pwllheli workings. One day, No. 76040 had an extra heavy load and was provided with a pilot. Two engines blasting around the coast was an impressive sight.

Machynlleth shed had an allocation of both these types in 1966, used for passenger and freight. It also had visitors from places like Shrewsbury and the busy Croes Newydd shed at Wrexham. Here they had time to make their engines look spotless, as No. 75047 arrived highly polished and looking a picture. So did Machynlleth use it straightaway on the Cambrian Coast Express? Well actually no, because they preferred No. 75016, which hid its green paint under a healthy layer of grime but ran like clockwork. In contrast to the gleam on No. 75047, Machynlleth had No. 76043, a sad and rusty old wreck. Eight weeks before I saw her she had arrived optimistically from Saltley shed in Birmingham, but after inspecting her the Machynlleth shed team simply pushed her into a siding and marked her for scrap.

The Cambrian line wasn't all steam, however. Diesel multiple units were making an appearance in 1966 and by the summer of 1967 they had vanquished the steam fleet. The best steamers went to north-west England to fight another day. The casualties joined No. 76043 and headed for the cutter's torch. So what of No. 75047 and its immaculate paintwork? Well, she lasted another year, but so did grubby No. 75016; both then had an appointment with the scrap man.

We've already mentioned Aberystwyth and its interchange between standard and narrow gauge. This won it a special place in our affections, as did Machynlleth with its elegant buildings that do duty to this day. But best of all was Morfa Mawddach, which stood (and still does) at the southern end of the 700-metre-long Barmouth Bridge, a wooden structure carrying trains, walkers and cyclists. Once a junction, Morfa Mawddach had lost its Ruabon connection in 1966 but was still busy, mainly with steam. It also had a truly excellent community bar, where the locals would mingle with visitors to relax before retiring. Sometimes we were distracted by trains coming past, but overall it was a fine place to reflect on the day's events. Sipping a well-earned pint of ale as a Class 4 pulls away with a couple of coaches is a funny kind of heaven, but it works for me.

The Pwllheli portion of the Cambrian Coast Express runs across Barmouth Bridge on 26 August 1966. This 2-6-0 was in charge of the service every day during this week, linking up with the Aberystwyth portion at Dovey Junction.

On 22 August 1966, when I took this picture, No. 75010 was part of the allocation at Croes Newydd, but she had been delivered new to Patricroft in 1951. Here she prepares to leave Machynlleth on an eastbound freight. Despite her scruffy condition, she lasted almost to the end of 1967.

No. 75002 was delivered new to the Western Region and painted in lined green livery. Here she stands respectably clean on Machynlleth shed on 22 August 1966 after being coaled, with a youthful fireman (slightly inappropriately dressed) on this warm day (all firemen seemed to be youthful at the end of steam).

Looking very smart, Standard Class 4 4-6-0 No. 75047 stands on Machynlleth shed on 22 August 1966 in lined black livery. She's a visitor from Croes Newydd Depot at Wrexham, who clearly still employed engine cleaners.

Despite the loss of her front numberplate, Class 4 4-6-0 No. 75055 is looking tidy at Machynlleth shed on 22 August 1966 with 2-6-0 No. 76040 alongside. She was a local engine at this time, but is here carrying a Mold Junction (6A) shed plate. No. 75055 was re-allocated three more times before withdrawal in May 1967.

It's another wonderful morning and we are at Fairbourne. A freight passes through the little station, headed by shabby green Standard Class 4 No. 75009 on 26 August 1966. Note the camping coach in the station.

Each day, No. 76040 hauled the Pwllheli portion of the Cambrian Coast Express and then worked its way back to Pwllheli on a stopping train late in the afternoon. This service is seen here at Morfa Mawddach station on 26 August 1966 and the sun has annoyingly popped behind the clouds.

This low angle makes No. 76040 look powerful as it passes a signal at Fairbourne after making a station stop in August 1966.

A perfect Welsh morning with the Pwllheli portion of the Cambrian Coast Express in the hands of BR Standard Class 4 2-6-0 No. 76040. This train is seen between Morfa Mawddach and Fairbourne.

Once confined to the London section of the Great Central, No. 76040 gets a taste of the mountain air south of Fairbourne station with the Up Cambrian Coast Express on 26 August 1966. (Bryan Jeyes)

Here we have a train from Pwllheli crossing the Barmouth Bridge on the morning of 25 August 1966. In charge is a Standard Class 4 2-6-0 and a seagull has flown right over the bridge. This is again the Pwllheli portion of the Cambrian Coast Express.

Aberystwyth station on 24 August 1966, with 4-6-0 No. 75014 shunting tank wagons.

Minffordd is well known as a station on the Festiniog Railway, but it has a British Railways station as well. Here we see a Metro Cammell DMU on 20 August 1967.

Standard 4-6-0 No. 75016 arrives at Machynlleth on a perfect summer day, 24 August 1966. The engine is very dirty but was actually in green livery. The train is the Up Cambrian Coast Express. Crews preferred this mechanically excellent engine to the gleaming No. 75047, which was available having worked in from Croes Newydd.

A Metro Cammell multiple unit at Minffordd station in August 1967. This was an interchange with the Festiniog Railway, which was quite important before Blaenau Ffestiniog was reopened. Notice the Davies Brothers slate works on the left, with piles of slate outside and a siding. This old established Porthmadog company was, I believe, still sending slate by rail when this picture was taken.

A Metro Cammell multiple unit arrives at Machynlleth from the east in August 1966, with a Standard Class 4 manoeuvring in the background. (Bryan Jeyes)

Standards gathered at Machynlleth shed in August 1966. No. 76043 (right) had arrived recently from Saltley in Birmingham, but was quickly deemed to be a lost cause and parked up for withdrawal. (Bryan Jeyes)

A perfect day in glorious Welsh scenery as a Standard 4-6-0 passes Porthmadog with a Shrewsbury to Pwllheli freight in August 1966.

Minffordd GWR station, which is reached from the Festiniog under a bridge and up a ramp. (Bryan Jeyes)

Some stations last for years after being closed and Dinas Mawddwy is an example. The 6-mile branch line from Cemmes Road station had closed to passengers back in 1931 but here in 1966 it stood as a splendid monument to a long-lost railway, and indeed exists today as a private house. (Bryan Jeyes)

Conclusion

Fifty years have passed since these railway holidays in Wales took place. They say you can never repeat the past, but I wonder. Of course, lots of things have changed. You can't have a beer at Morfa Mawddach station and you won't see No. 75016 arriving in the sunshine at Machynlleth on the Cambrian Coast Express, but at least the station is still open. You can enjoy a ride behind *Prince*, *Llywelyn*, *Linda*, *Dolgoch* and *The Earl*. What's more, you no longer have to walk to Blaenau Ffestiniog as the train will take you there. You can still go to the top of Snowdon, potter along on the Fairbourne to get a ferry and ride up the Rheidol valley. Enjoy the Welsh Highland as well (but don't invest in it). Suggesting you cancel that cruise is a big ask … maybe you can do both?

Bibliography

Books

Boyd, J. I. C., *Narrow Gauge Railways in Mid-Wales* (Lingfield: The Oakwood Press, 1965).
Boyd, J. I. C., *Narrow Gauge Railways in South Caernarvonshire Volume 2* (Oxford: The Oakwood Press, 1989).
Davies, W. K. J., *abc Narrow Gauge Railways* (London: Ian Allan, 1961).
Hollingsworth, B., *Ffestiniog Adventure* (Newton Abbot: David & Charles, 1981).
Lee, C. E., *The Welsh Highland Railway* (Dawlish: David & Charles, 1962).
Rolt, L. T. C., *Railway Adventure* (Dawlish: David & Charles, 1961).
Whitehouse, P. B., *Festiniog Railway Revival* (London: Ian Allan, 1963).

Websites

The Fairbourne Steam Railway, www.fairbournerailway.com/index
The Vale of Rheidol Railway, www.rheidolrailway.co.uk

Also available from Amberley Publishing

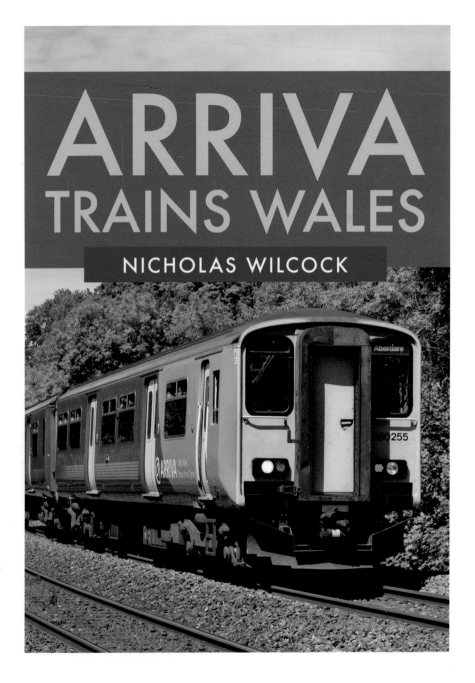

Available from all good bookshops or to order direct
Please call **01453-847-800**
www.amberley-books.com